KENDRA,
I FOUND TH[IS BOO]K
INSPIRING [AND THOUGHT]
YOU MIGHT LIK[E IT TOO.]
XOXO,
KK

THE FOURTH WAVE

© 2018 Jennifer Armbrust

All rights reserved. No part of this book may be reproduced, stored in a retrieval system, or transmitted in any form or by any means, electronic, mechanical, photocopying, recording or otherwise without the prior permission of the publisher.

Published by The Fourth Wave
P.O. Box 1433, Topanga, CA 90290
thefourthwaveisfeminine.com

This is an updated version of the "Proposals for the Feminine Economy" lecture, commissioned by CreativeMornings and presented June 17, 2015 at the Portland Art Museum.

Design: Jennifer Armbrust

ISBN: 978 1 7336353 0 1

Distributed by Sister
sister.is

10 9 8 7 6 5 4 3 2

PROPOSALS FOR THE FEMININE ECONOMY

JENNIFER ARMBRUST

**A DREAM
YOU DREAM
ALONE IS
ONLY
A DREAM.**

**A DREAM
YOU DREAM
TOGETHER
IS REALITY.**

— YOKO ONO

THE PROPOSALS

BUSINESS AS ART	11
THE FOURTH WAVE IS FEMININE	21
100 WAYS TO MAKE MORE MONEY	27
THE FEMININE ECONOMY	31
FEMINIST ENTREPRENEURSHIP	44
12 PRINCIPLES	55
MONEY FOLLOWS VALUE	85
NOTES	92

I WANT TO START BY TAKING A FEW MOMENTS TO GET PRESENT IN OUR BODIES

First, notice that you're breathing.

Take a few nice, full, easy breaths. You take about 20,000 breaths per day. Begin to notice a few of them.

Feel your feet on the floor.
Feel your seat on your chair.
Feel the chair holding you.

You sit on the chair, the chair is supported by the floor, and the floor is supported by the foundation of the building which is supported by the earth.

There's an entire world under your feet, down there in the soil. There are worms and roots and insects and rhizomes and millions of microorganisms. Just sitting here in your chair, you are connected to the earth and all these living beings.

BUSINESS AS ART

In 2003, when I was 25 years old, I opened my first business, an art gallery in Portland, Oregon called Motel. Over the course of five years, I produced over 50 exhibitions and worked with over 100 artists.

I did not come from an art history, gallery, or business administration background. I was a punk kid from Olympia, Washington who fell in love with art. I was raised in an underground music scene founded on the belief that we make our own culture. I was driven by raw D.I.Y. spirit, and initially, very naive to business—especially, the business of art.

Motel was a practice in improvisation, innovation, and determination.

Through my time as a gallerist, I learned that the key to a successful art career is a regular studio practice. You cannot *create* inspiration, right? And the harder you try, usually the more elusive it becomes. You can only create *space* for ideas to arrive.

The job of the artist is to show up everyday in the studio, pick up her tools, and see what happens. A successful artist will define a set of rules or conditions for her process. She will rely on instinct over intellect. The value of her work lies in her ability to communicate her singular world view in a meaningful way. And to do this, she must take risks.

I am an artist. My business is my studio. I show up and make space for ideas to arrive. I use rules and limitations as creative constraints. I lead with intuition. I create value for my business by uniquely expressing my ideas and beliefs. I am constantly taking risks.

Like any committed artist, I'm driven by a persistent preoccupation. The central question I'm investigating through my work is—

CAN I SURVIVE ON MY OWN TERMS, WITH MY PERSONAL & CREATIVE INTEGRITY INTACT?

Let's go deeper into this idea of
business as art.

Anyone in business knows that it's a highly creative environment.

BUT, DOES THAT MAKE IT ART?

I came up with some definitions for us to work with.

WHAT IS BUSINESS?

Business is an experiment in survival involving money and the creative impulse.

WHAT IS ART?

Art is the unique expression of an emotion or an idea, wherein something is at stake.

WHAT IS BUSINESS AS ART?

An experiment in survival involving money, the creative impulse, and the unique expression of an emotion or idea, wherein something is at stake.

WHAT IS AT STAKE?

FEMININE-ISM

THE FOURTH WAVE IS FEMININE

I've long been interested in gender and economics. My undergraduate degree is in Critical Theory which encompasses feminist theory, critical race theory, Marxist philosophy, post-structuralist and post-modern theory, and postcolonial theory.

During my time in the academy, I was fascinated with the study of *power*—what it is, how it flows, and strategies for redistributing it.

Upon leaving college, my theoretical fascinations largely went into hibernation until 2015, when I was asked to give a talk on *Revolution*. With twelve years of entrepreneurship and five businesses under my belt, I found myself in an exciting moment of integration. My persistent passions, my ideological fascinations, and my love of feminist theory collided with my business acumen and seven years of healing arts training.

I REALIZED THAT BY APPLYING FEMININE & FEMINIST PRINCIPLES TO ECONOMICS & BUSINESS I COULD GIVE BIRTH TO A NEW FRAMEWORK FOR ENTRE-PRENEURSHIP.

After I shuttered the gallery, I moved to New York City for one long, dark year. I came back to Portland depressed and depleted, so I immersed myself in self-help and healing studies.

I began working with an intuitive counselor, a woman with the ability to read auras and chakras. Liliana Barzola mentored me in healing arts for eight subsequent years, teaching me tools and techniques for working with energy while bringing me into her mission to heal and evolve the feminine archetype.

Around this time, my friend Lisa Radon introduced me to the word *feminine-ism* and everything coalesced.

YES!

This was the concept I'd been looking for. Not a celebration of all things girly or a sexualization of womanhood. But rather, a valuation of feminine *characteristics* such as empathy, receptivity, nurturing, introspection, and gentleness.

If we view the patriarchy not as *men* dominating *women*, but as *masculine* dominance and *feminine* subjugation, we notice that not just women but all feminized subjects are dominated, devalued, discredited, or controlled. Consider that money, water, the moon, mysticism and witchcraft, and the earth also belong to the feminine archetype and we see that patriarchy is not just concerned with controlling female bodies, but feminine symbols as well.

Women have traditionally been the carriers of the feminine, but it doesn't belong to them alone. In a healthy and balanced world, all humans would embody masculine and feminine qualities fluidly and in unique balance, regardless of their sex organs.

However, currently, collectively (in America, at least), we are missing half of our gender vocabulary. Both men and women are very practiced at personifying masculine qualities, which are often codified as *power* and *success*. But are generally uncomfortable embodying feminine characteristics—especially in business—because they don't want to be perceived as weak, vulnerable, or inadequate.

To create a gender-fluid future, we need to heal our other half.

The present moment calls for a widespread celebration and reclamation of the feminine archetype.

FEMININE-ISM

The fourth wave of feminism.

With these insights and this exciting new concept of *feminine-ism*, I began bringing feminine principles into my business consulting practice.

Fortuitously, I was asked to contribute to Day Job, an anthology of writing by women on creative work. This gave me the opportunity to play with these ideas and to articulate my thinking.

I wrote *100 Ways to Make More Money: Proposals for the Feminine Economy*. It was simultaneously a manifesto, a question, a healing, a critique of Capitalism, and a distillation of all the advice I'd been given around work, happiness, and money.

100 WAYS TO MAKE MORE MONEY

PROPOSALS FOR THE FEMININE ECONOMY

1 Drink water. 2 Go to bed on time. 3 Create more opportunities for people to give you money. 4 Graciously and gratefully receive gifts. 5 Balance your checkbook, weekly. 6 Go everywhere you're invited. 7 Ask for what you need. 8 Nurture your relationships. 9 Slow down. 10 Invite your heroes to lunch. 11 Volunteer your time and talents to projects you believe in. 12 Make a list of everything you're good at. 13 Tell people exactly how to utilize you. 14 Don't waste time trying to master what you're not good at. 15 Make no assumptions. 16 Have no expectations. 17 Improvise. 18 Be resourceful. Remember! You have everything you need. 19 Surprise yourself by saying yes when you usually say no. 20 Give meaningful gifts. 21 Tell the truth. 22 Talk numbers. 23 Say how you're feeling. 24 Read Karl Marx. 25 Connect with someone you love, daily. 26 Begin doing everything you know you should be doing. 27 Stop doing the things you know you shouldn't be doing. 28 Nourish yourself and others.

29 Communicate clearly. 30 Reply to phone calls and emails promptly. 31 Send hand-written thank you notes. 32 Verbally acknowledge others' efforts, talents, generosity, and courage. 33 Remember, what other people think of you isn't your business. 34 Forgive everybody, all the time. 35 Presume innocence. 36 Be transparent about your desires and motivations. 37 Let yourself want what you want, no matter how big or small. 38 Visualize your magical future. 39 Utilize the public library. 40 Read more books. 41 Be thankful. 42 Keep a regular schedule. 43 Show up. 44 Unplug on weekends and holidays. 45 Tell the people you love why you love them. 46 Rest when you are tired, eat when you are hungry. 47 Embrace vulnerability. 48 Practice courage & compassion in the face of fear. 49 Start a nest egg. Feed it regularly. 50 Get more houseplants or plant a garden. 51 Think about the people who make the things you buy and use. 52 Visualize money as water—consider how it flows. 53 Give money to buskers and panhandlers. 54 Remember, we're all in this together. 55 Host a potluck or dinner party. 56 Know exactly how much money you have. 57 Know exactly how much debt you have. 58 Keep imagining abundance. 59 Wake up early. 60 Exercise. 61 Pay taxes, gladly. 62 Read the newspaper daily. 63 Notice your assumptions about rich people. 64 Notice your assumptions about poor people. 65 Become a better listener, ask more questions. 66 Maintain eye contact. 67 Stop judging everyone all the time. 68 Practice radical receptivity. 69 Notice when you feel the need to hoard or protect what you have.

70 Breathe. 71 Spend more time in nature. 72 Play hooky from work at least four times a year. 73 Go for a walk. 74 Touch and talk to the plants. 75 Know your worth. Know that this has nothing to do with how much money you have. 76 Forgive yourself for all the times you've devalued yourself. 77 Say no to work you don't believe in. 78 Trust your intuition. 79 See fiscal empowerment as a revolutionary act. 80 Become conscious—know why you do what you do with money. 81 Consider what fiscal responsibility means to you. 82 Write about any shame you feel around money. 83 Talk freely about finances with friends and family. 84 Make choices in alignment with your personal honor code. 85 Act with intention. 86 Do what you say you are going to do. 87 Put your money where your heart is—support the people, businesses, and organizations you value. 88 Stop spending money at businesses you don't respect. 89 Prioritize your health and wellness, even if it requires sacrifice or discipline. 90 Feed yourself the best quality food available. 91 Shop at the farmer's market whenever possible. Make friends with the farmers. 92 Stop eating foods your body doesn't like. 93 Purge the things in your life you don't need, use, or want. 94 Give unwanted goods to charity or have a garage sale. 95 Get a dog. Or a cat. Or a child. Or a lover, if you don't have one already. 96 Make friends with your neighbors. 97 Call your family. 98 Experience the joy of letting people help you. 99 Count your blessings. See how high you can go. 100 Talk more about what you love.

PROPOSALS FOR THE FEMININE ECONOMY

What I was trying to do with *100 Ways* was to create a new vision of wealth and value by offering provocations under the auspices of how to make more money. I wrote it intuitively, without the intention of developing a larger framework. It was a playful experiment: alchemizing feminine principles and conventional business wisdom.

While *100 Ways* helped me to gather my thinking, it didn't present a cogent articulation of what a Feminine Economy might look like and why it's necessary. So, I'd like to do that now.

WHAT IS AN ECONOMY?

An economy is a system that determines worth and allocation.

WHAT IS CAPITALISM?

Capitalism is both an economic system (defined by private ownership of the means of production and their operation for profit) and a worldview, an ideology.

WHEN I DISSECT THE IDEALS OF CAPITALISM— *ITS IDEOLOGY—* **IT SEEMS TO ME TO BE A VERY MASCULINE ECONOMY.**

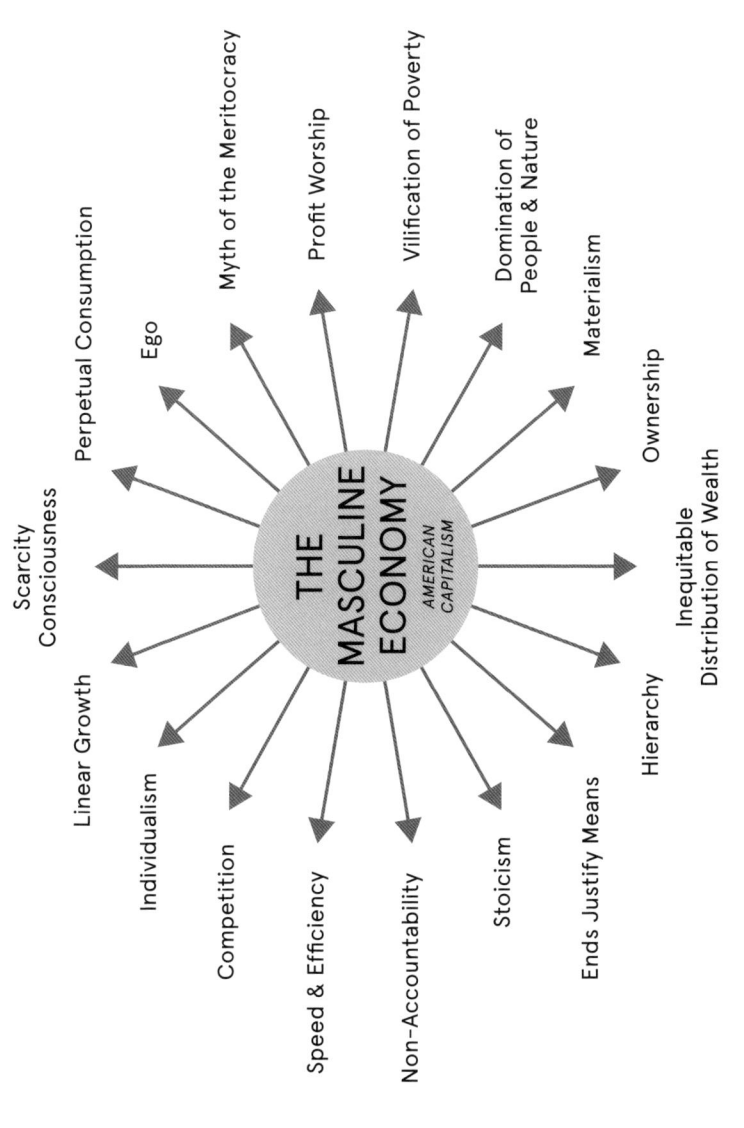

IF CAPITALISM IS AN ECONOMY THAT VALUES MASCULINE TRAITS, WHAT COULD ANOTHER ECONOMY LOOK LIKE?

THE FEMININE ECONOMY

- Gratitude
- Integrity
- Honesty
- Connecting with Nature
- Empathy
- Care
- Asking Questions
- Sustainability
- Intimacy
- Embodiment
- Generosity
- Ease
- Collaboration
- Interdependence
- Cyclical Growth
- Abundance Consciousness
- Resourcefulness
- Mindfulness

THE FEMININE ECONOMY PROPOSES A NEW SET OF ECONOMIC VALUES AND A REDISTRIBUTION OF MONEY AND POWER, BASED ON FEMININE PRINCIPLES.

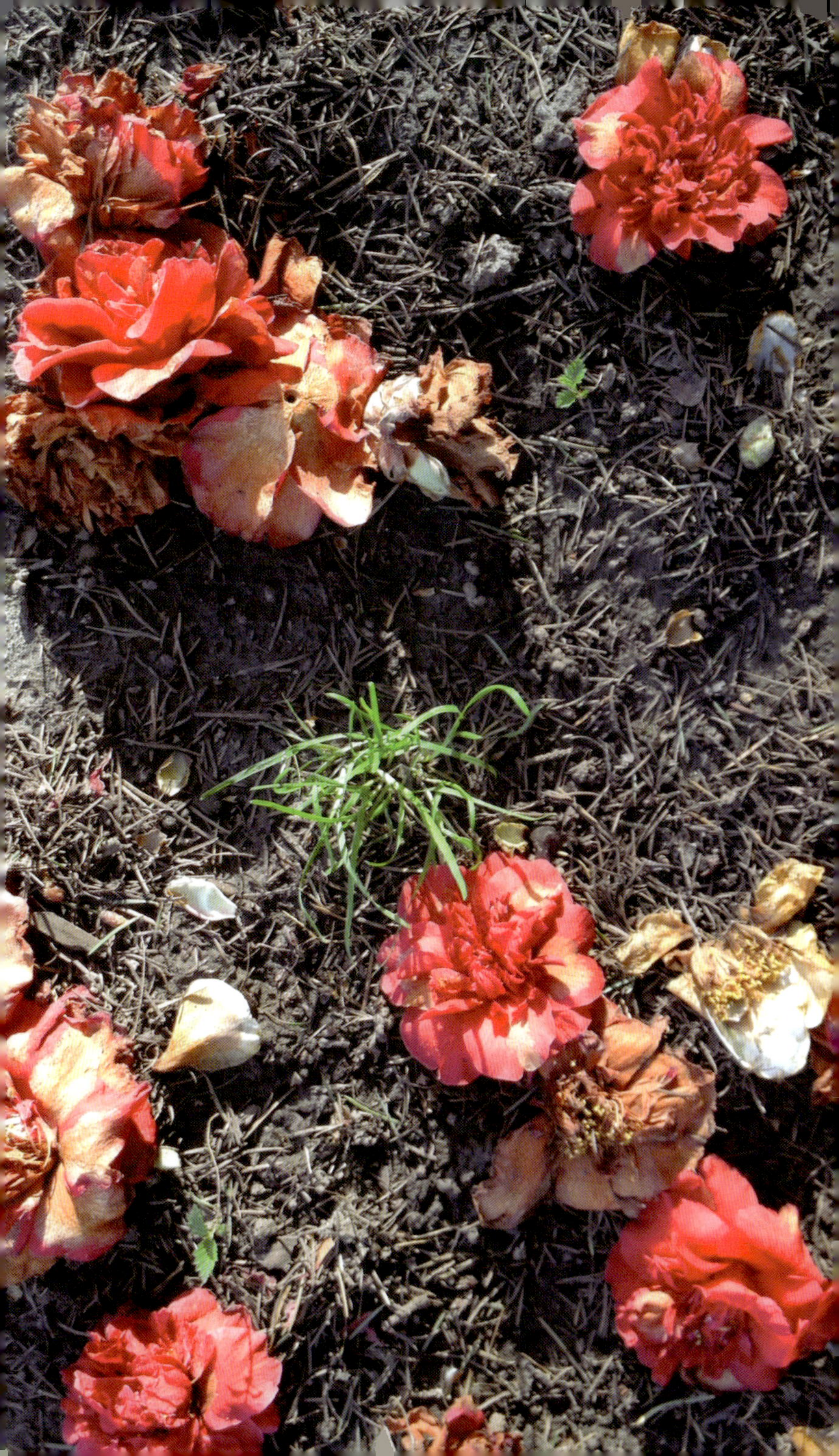

WHY? WHY DO WE NEED A NEW ECONOMY? DOESN'T THE ONE WE HAVE WORK JUST FINE?

Citing current conditions, including extreme wealth disparity, Citizen's United, the man-made famine in Yemen, floods and raging wildfires exacerbated by climate change, the Dakota Access Pipeline, price gouging for prescription medications, stagnant wages, prison slave labor, the militarization of America, and private contractors putting immigrant children into cages, to name a few, I would argue—

CAPITALISM IS NOT WORKING

AM I PROPOSING CONSCIOUS CAPITALISM?

No, again. We know from scholarship as old as Marx and as recent as Piketty that Capitalism inherently breeds inequality.

I'M PROPOSING BUSINESS AS A SITE TO EMBODY OUR VALUES, CREATE NEW ECONOMIES, & EXPERIMENT WITH NEW DISTRIBUTIONS OF POWER & RESOURCES.

Through iteration, experimentation, and innovation—in other words, treating *business as art*— it is possible that we will find a way out of the dysfunction of where we are now and into something new.

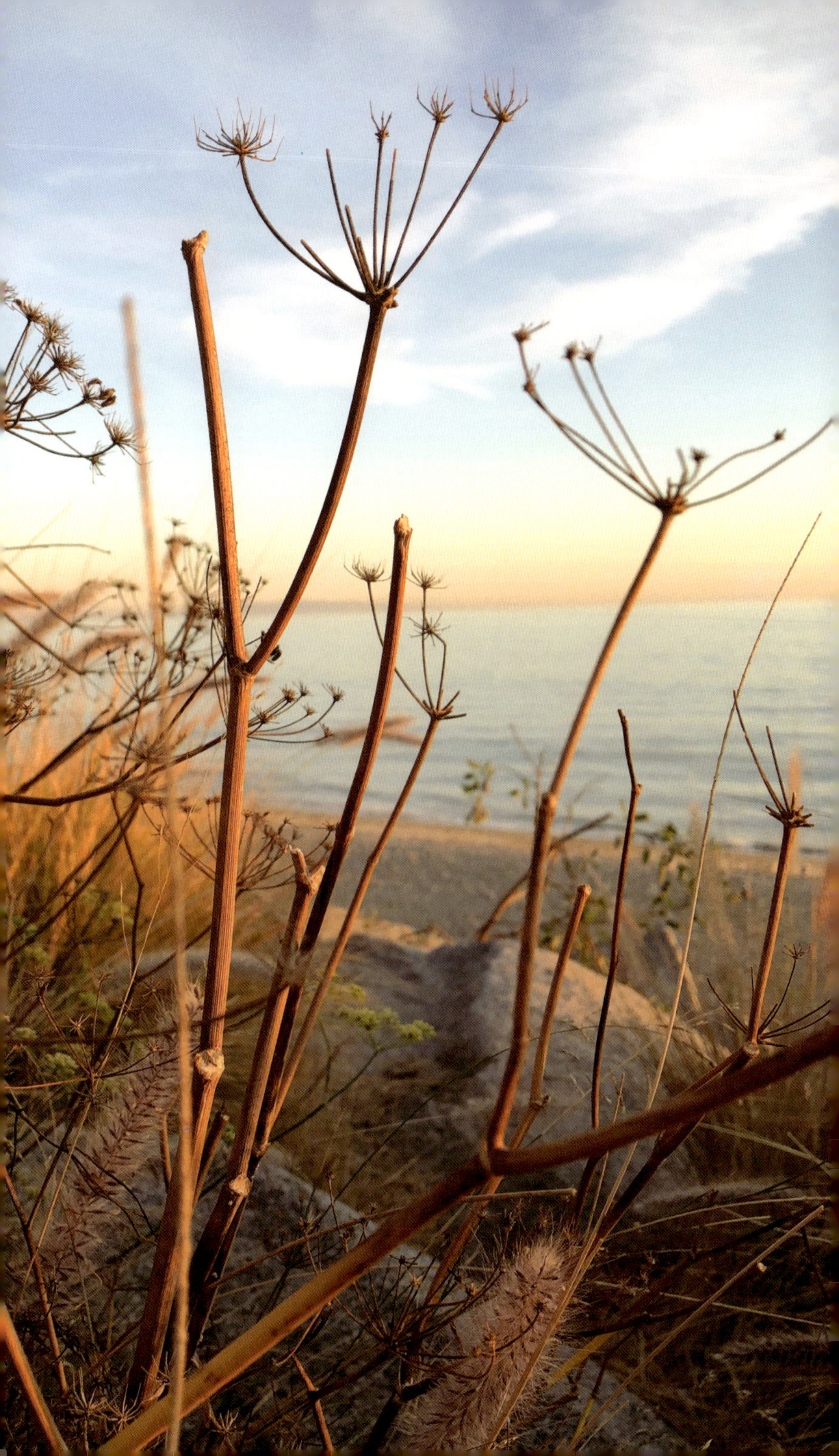

FEMINIST ENTREPRENEURSHIP

HOW DO WE TRANSLATE THESE IDEALS INTO PRACTICE? HOW DO WE MAKE THE FEMININE ECONOMY REAL?

Before we get into practicalities, let's take a few minutes to remember what feminism is and why it matters.

I recently met with a client who wanted to know if her business was feminist by fact of her being a woman.

Put bluntly: No.

Being a woman doesn't automatically make you a feminist. Being a woman and running a business doesn't automatically make your business a feminist business. *Feminist* does not equal *woman* and *woman* does not equal *feminist*, or these words would be synonyms and they're not.

For example, 52% of white women voted for Trump.

Feminism has a socio-political agenda. It is not a brand or a style or a trend. It's not about t-shirts. It's a multi-generational movement committed to consciousness, empowerment, empathy, and importantly, to actively dismantling myriad systemic, institutionalized, normalized, interpersonal, and internalized oppressions.

bell hooks is a leading feminist thinker. I love her work because it is heartfelt, brilliant, accessible, and intersectional—meaning, she articulates how race, class, sexuality, gender, nationality, ability, and other identities, *intersect* to differently shape a woman's access to power.

hooks gives us an incredibly useful and succinct definition of feminism—

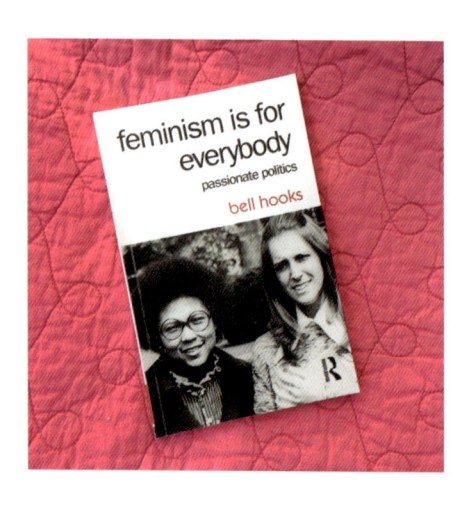

SIMPLY PUT, FEMINISM IS A MOVEMENT TO END SEXISM, SEXIST EXPLOITATION, AND OPPRESSION.

— bell hooks

WHAT DOES THIS MEAN IN A BUSINESS CONTEXT?

This requires that we, as feminists and entrepreneurs, develop our critical consciousness. It necessitates that we engage with questions of sexism and exploitation, of racism, classism, elitism, and accessibility in our own businesses and in the broader business paradigm.

Feminist entrepreneurship asks us to take a hard look at the world around us—at our society and culture, at our institutions and government, at our communities, at our relationships (including our relationship with ourselves), and especially at our businesses—to find the places we are complicit with, or even actively perpetuating (often unknowingly) sexism and other forms of oppression.

Feminist entrepreneurship also requires that we quit equating masculine principles with *success* and *power*, and feminine principles with *inadequacy* and *weakness*.

To do something as audacious as call your business "feminist" requires showing up every day with humility, heart, intrepid creativity, criticality, courage, self-love, & a passion for growth. It requires accountability to yourself, your business, and to the larger social project of dismantling patriarchal & oppressive systems.

FEMINIST ENTREPRENEURSHIP IS NOT A THING YOU ACHIEVE,

IT'S A THING YOU COMMIT TO.

A business gives you the opportunity to create something bigger than yourself. Feminist entrepreneurship isn't just concerned with personal growth or creating an isolated utopia within your company. It's about *social* change. It's about identifying the larger impact you can make through your company, the legacy you will leave in your community and the world.

When we remember that there are well over 200 years of feminist scholarship, it becomes clear that to distill all of those insights and wisdom into a workable framework for entrepreneurship is going to take some time. We won't figure it out overnight. And, I can't do it alone.

However, as a starting point, I've attempted to identify a set of core tenets for feminist entrepreneurship. The *12 Principles for Prototyping a Feminist Business* serve as my framework for this project—a road map for making the Feminine Economy real.

I consider the *Principles* a working draft. I invite you to use them, to modify them, and to write your own rules for feminist entrepreneurship.

12 PRINCIPLES FOR PROTOTYPING A FEMINIST BUSINESS

1. You have a body.
2. You are connected with the earth, the plants, and all living beings.
3. Integrate!
4. Institutionalize empathy: build frameworks that support feelings.
5. Embody your values.
6. Reclaim happiness: new definitions of success.
7. Consider everything an experiment.
8. Free yourself from the myth of the meritocracy.
9. Tell the truth.
10. Cultivate abundance consciousness.
11. A business can be a healing for yourself & others.
12. A business can be a model for a new social & economic order.

☺ Jennifer Armbrust, Sister. *sister.is*

12 PRINCIPLES FOR PROTOTYPING A FEMINIST BUSINESS

I
YOU
HAVE
A
BODY

Your body does not want to work 60 hours a week. It does not want to sit all day. Your body may get sick or need a doctor. Your body might want to go to the beach. Your body craves nourishing food and rest and movement. Your body delights in pleasure and play.

The sex and gender of your body affect if you are listened to and taken seriously. The abilities of your body determine your physical access to spaces, resources, and experiences. The color of your skin impacts your access to funding when you seek to launch or grow your business.

Capitalism, business, our egos all tell us to override our body's needs and its messages in the name of productivity and profit. This alienates us from our joy, our presence, and our intuition. It can also lead to illness, injury, addiction, and persistent fatigue.

Create business structures that support and nourish your body and all the other bodies you know.

2
YOU ARE CONNECTED WITH THE EARTH, THE PLANTS, & ALL LIVING BEINGS

Mama Earth is our primary co-creative partner, and yet we take her so easily for granted*!* Everything above you, below you, around you came from the earth.

When we are alienated from the earth, we forget her incredible wealth and regenerative abilities, as well as her gifts of nourishment, support, and healing. We fall into scarcity and competition. We also create mindless waste, become unconscious consumers, and engage business practices that deplete and damage her. This is unnecessary.

You are in-relationship with the earth. What kind of partner have you been in the past? What kind of partner do you want to be to her in the future?

Touch the plants. Talk to the animals. Lie on the ground. Dig your fingers in the dirt. Feel the unconditional support the earth is always already giving to you.

Envision your shared future. Express your love and gratitude through stewardship and care.

Commune.

3
INTEGRATE!

Integrity is another word for *honor*. To be integrated is to feel whole. When you live in alignment with your values you experience peace because you have self-respect. You don't have to judge or regret your actions because they were made with conscious awareness and intent.

You have the opportunity to craft a business that allows to you be fully yourself—integrating your passions, your wisdom, your talents, your beliefs, your idiosyncrasies, your persistent preoccupations, your pleasures, and your purpose.

Often, when we go to work in a traditional job, we leave a part of ourselves at the door. What if your business allowed you, and everyone else within it, to show up fully as you are? *How would that feel?*

Gather all your parts. Leave nothing behind.
Make your business a site of integration.
Make it a home.

4 INSTITUTIONALIZE EMPATHY: BUILD FRAMEWORKS THAT SUPPORT FEELINGS

Empathy is not sympathy. Sympathy keeps us centered in our personal experience and allows us to indulge our own feelings in response to another's experience. It enables us to keep a safe distance from pain, discomfort, anger, and trauma.

Empathy is different. Empathy requires us to do enough self-work that we can get beyond our own ego and be fully, truly present with another's experience. Empathy is the act of listening and understanding, with our full body and spirit, what someone else is feeling.

This principle requires us each to do the work of dismantling sexist and racist institutions and beliefs, in order to access our full empathetic capacities. It demands that we take accountability for our unearned privileges, and embark upon the process of healing our individual and collective traumas, as well as our internalized oppressions.

Attunement to feelings—our own and others'—guides us to the fulfillment of needs. The ongoing fulfillment of needs is the foundation of a sustainable life. (And business*!* And world*!*)

5
EMBODY YOUR VALUES

The Masculine Economy has its own values and espoused virtues to serve its ends of consolidated profit and power. Many people unconsciously adopt these ideals as their own, while others falsely believe they must compromise their own principles and live by these rules in order to survive.

Thriving economically while living your *own* values is deeply disruptive to the current social and economic order.

Cultivate your inner authority. Build structures and practices in alignment with your values and deeply-held beliefs. Support others who do the same.

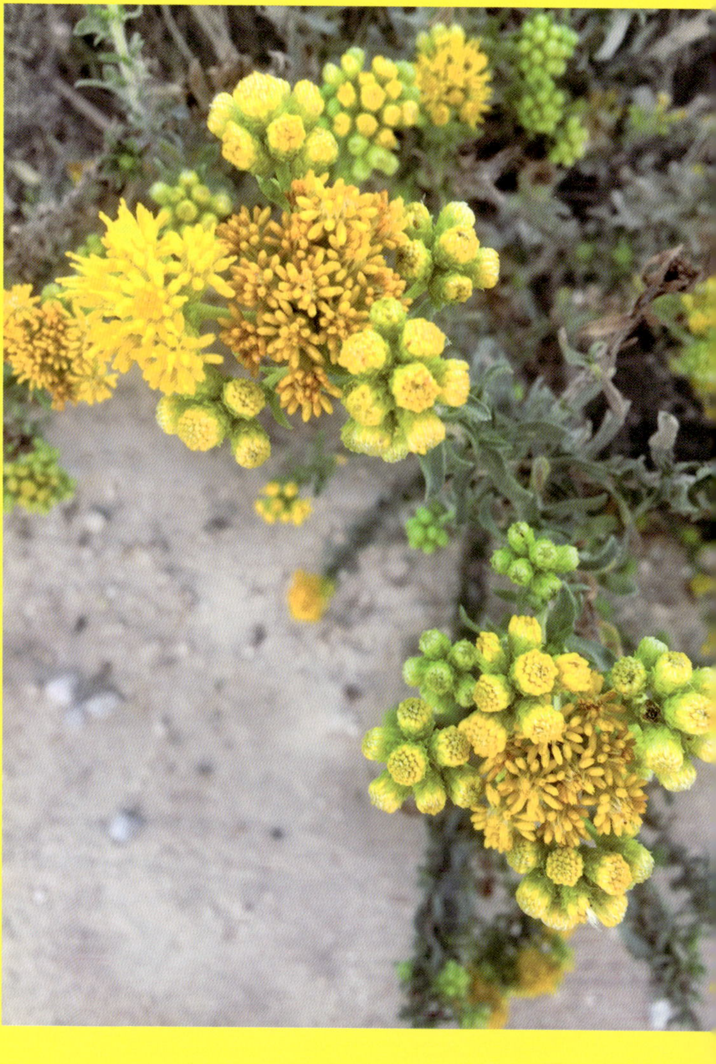

6
RECLAIM HAPPINESS: MAKE NEW DEFINITIONS OF SUCCESS

This principle sounds nice but this one will gut you, because the old *you* that was created by society, others' expectations, and inherited beliefs, must die so you can begin to live your life on your own terms.

Seek happiness, pleasure, and the fulfillment of needs. Move towards the things that bring you nourishment and joy.

Call back your power from the people and ideas you have given it away to, and reclaim it from those who have taken it without your consent.

Release the life you were told you would, could, or should have, and imagine anew.

Practice trusting yourself above all else.

The key to happiness is:
do things that make you happy.

7
CONSIDER EVERYTHING AN EXPERIMENT

Do not wait until you know to act. Anything you don't know, you will learn in the process.

Improvise.
Iterate.
Ask questions.
Ask more questions.
Explore!
Give yourself permission to not know and to make mistakes.
Find freedom in uncertainty.
Be receptive and responsive instead of predictive and protective.

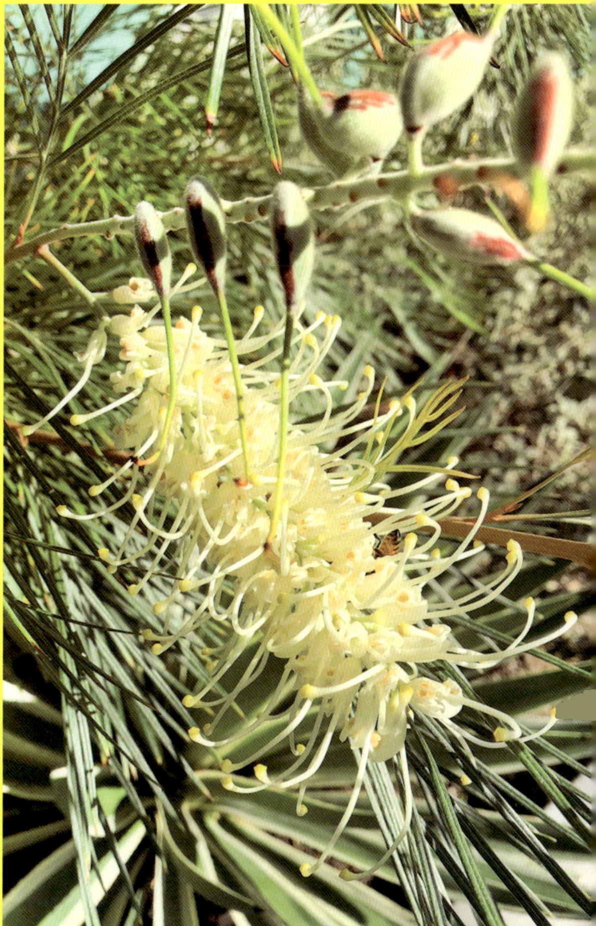

8
FREE YOURSELF FROM THE MYTH OF THE MERITOCRACY

Capitalism loves the meritocracy—the belief that your wealth, your happiness, and your value as a human being are rewards for your effort and *hard work*. The meritocracy conveniently ignores systemic racism and sexism, inherited wealth, that some bodies cannot "work" in a traditional sense, the Capitalist mechanics of class inequality, and all other structural factors that actually determine one's access to wealth and resources.

The meritocracy demands that you subjugate your needs (physical, emotional, spiritual) to productivity. It alienates you from the messages of your body and your intuition by insisting that wealth and happiness come from hard work.

This is a lie.

There is no earning. There's no deserving. There's no reward. Divest your ego of the need to prove itself through struggle, sacrifice, and hard work.

Ask yourself, *"Would it be alright with me if my life got easier?"*

Let it be easy.

9
TELL THE TRUTH

We are being so thoroughly lied to it's an epidemic. We must create businesses where words have deep meaning, aligned with action.

Reveal yourself.
Declare your beliefs.
Say how you're feeling.
Admit when you don't know.
Have courage!
Root out your denials.
Repudiate lies, deceptions,and misrepresentations.
Hold yourself and others accountable.
Own your skills, talents, & abilities.
Use your business to advocate for the people
and things you believe in.
Express your pleasure.
Speak your truth.

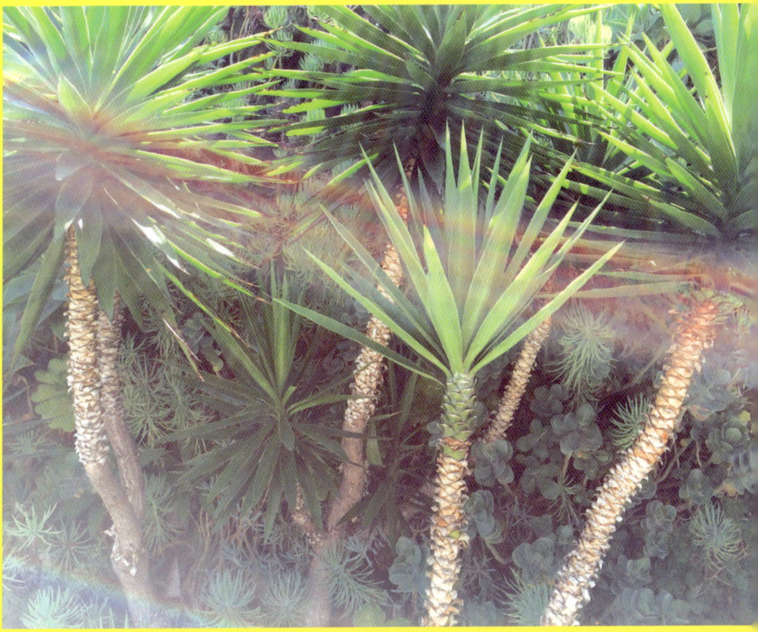

10
CULTIVATE ABUNDANCE CONSCIOUSNESS

Feel how rich you are already. Pause. Breathe.
Connect with the present moment. And feel how
rich you are *right now*.

Sense into your connection with the earth.
Nature is abundance embodied.

Accumulation is not the same as *abundance*.
Abundance is the felt sense of *enough*. It is feeling
nourished, and knowing that support is always
available when you need it.

Scarcity teaches us gratitude & responsibility.
Be grateful.

Learn the difference between your wants and
your needs.

Become a conscious steward of money—use it to
support the people, things, and ideas you believe
in so that they will flourish.

Remember, money isn't the only form
of wealth.

Nourish.
Nurture.
Savor.

11
A BUSINESS CAN BE A HEALING FOR YOURSELF & OTHERS

Everything that you are needing, someone else is needing, too. Everything that you are healing for yourself, you are healing for someone else, too.

Where are you most in need of healing right now? What is the medicine? How can you weave that into the fabric of your business so that as you heal yourself, you heal others, too?

Make your business a medicine, a salve.

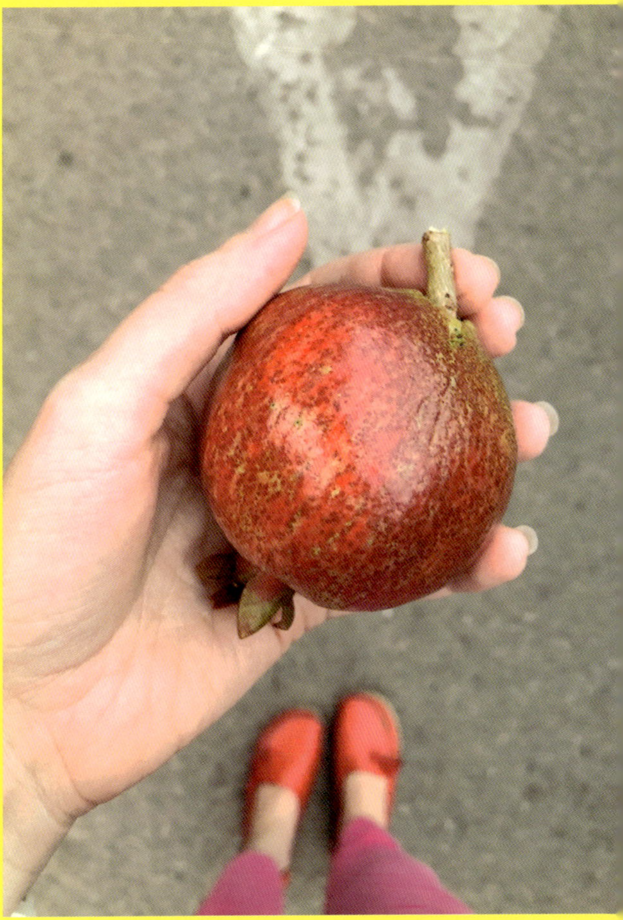

12
A BUSINESS CAN BE A MODEL FOR A NEW SOCIAL & ECONOMIC ORDER

As entrepreneurs, we have the opportunity to agitate the current social, political, and economic order by experimenting with new business models that honor our values, our humanity, and the earth. As we bring feminine and feminist principles into our business practices, we give birth to a new economic paradigm.

A FEMINIST BUSINESS CAN MODEL NEW WAYS OF LIVING, WORKING, AND BEING TOGETHER.

THIS IS ABOUT TRANSFORMING OUR RELATIONSHIP TO MONEY, TO WORK, TO THE EARTH, TO OUR BODIES, AND TO EACH OTHER.

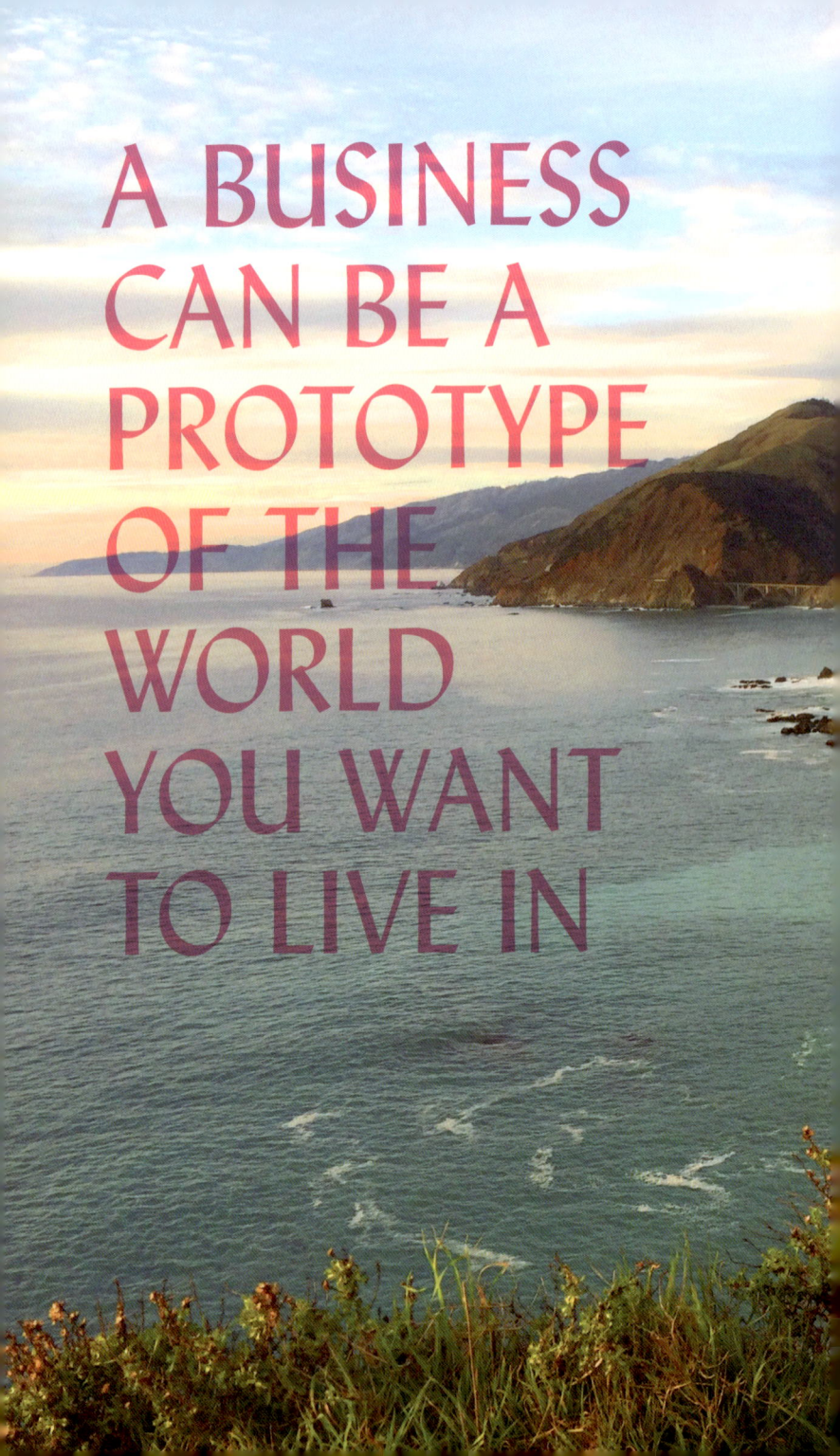

A BUSINESS CAN BE A PROTOTYPE OF THE WORLD YOU WANT TO LIVE IN

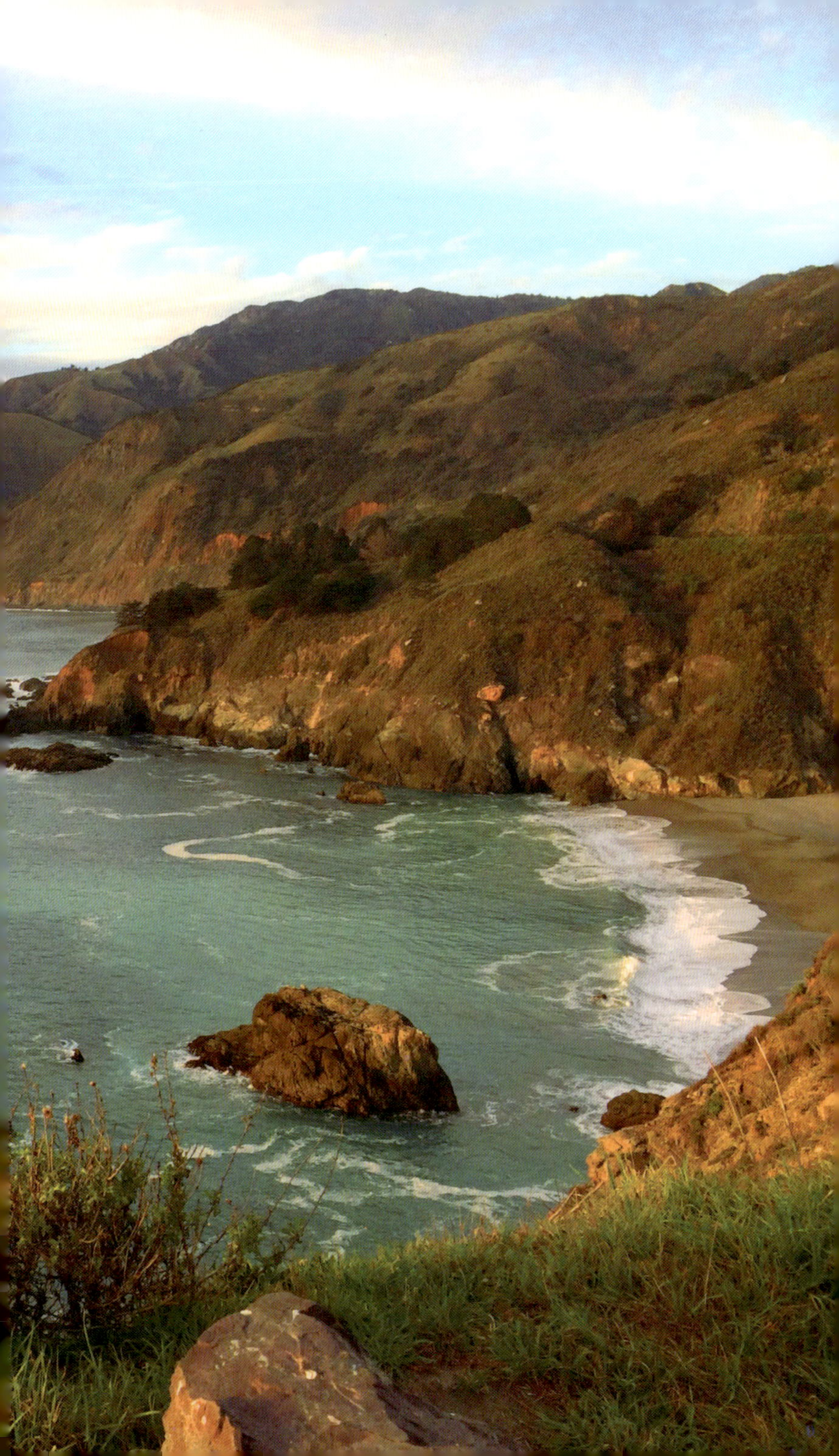

NEVER FOR MONEY
ALWAYS FOR LOVE

MONEY FOLLOWS VALUE

Collectively, we have been valuing masculine traits for so long it feels like the natural order. But it hasn't always been this way.

Money follows value. Or, said another way, money follows our *values*. As a culture, we have been placing high value on masculine traits. Accordingly, our economy rewards businesses and individuals who embody those qualities.

Collectively, we have been devaluing feminine characteristics for so long that they have little worth on the marketplace. (And also, women have been giving it away for free*!*)

Want money to flow towards the feminine? Start valuing feminine principles, not just intellectually, but in practice. Begin by celebrating and cultivating feminine qualities in yourself, your business, and in those around you, including men.

Business-as-usual reinforces white patriarchal dominance. We can refuse to participate in the overvaluation of masculine qualities by developing business practices that embody feminine principles.

We can own our power of abundance and become conscious stewards of wealth. We can experiment with redistributions of power and resources, using our businesses to prototype the world we want to live in. As we do so, we contribute to the larger feminist project.

Make your business a channel for resources and support to flow toward what you value and believe in, including yourself. As we honor feminine-ist principles in our business practices, we reshape the business archetype, liberating it from the shackles of the patriarchy. This is how we make the Feminine Economy real.

THE FEMININE ECONOMY

As we venture together into the uncharted territory of feminist entrepreneurship, we will unquestionably make mistakes, have blind spots, & grapple with constraints. That's okay. As long as we continue to take accountability for ourselves and practice forgiveness, we will learn and grow and find new ways.

The rewards are rich: self-love, integrity, a feeling of wholeness, a sense of purpose and efficacy, and a knowing that we are actively contributing to the project of a more compassionate and sane world.

The beauty & magic lies in the journey, not the destination. We make the road by walking.

NOTES

IX This meditation draws on "The Twelve-Phase Healing Trauma Program" by Peter Levine in *Healing Trauma: A Pioneering Program for Restoring the Wisdom of Your Body*, Sounds True, 2005.

27-29 Thanks to Taryn Cowart & Corbin LaMont for inviting me to contribute to *Day Job*. Woven into this piece are the words of many, including Clifton Burt, Sarah Fontaine, Marissa Mayer, Caroline Myss, Luna Jaffe, Liliana Barzola, Lynne Twist, Maria Nemeth, Kim Krans, & Max Fenton.

33 Turns out, it's hard to pin down exactly what Capitalism *IS*. Just ask an economist. This definition borrows from the Wikipedia entry on Capitalism.

37 I did not conduct any quantitative research in the development of *Proposals for the Feminine Economy*. However, if you are looking for analytical data on the rise and relevance of feminine qualities in 21st century leadership, you might like *The Athena Doctrine: How Women (and the Men Who Think Like Them) Will Rule The Future* by John Gerzema & Michael D'Antonio, Jossey-Bass, 2013.

40 For more on Capitalism and inequality, see *The Marx-Engels Reader*, edited by Robert C. Tucker, Norton, 1972. And *Capital in the Twenty-First Century* by Thomas Piketty, Belknap Press, 2014.

45 For two years following the 2016 election, the statistic of 52% of white women voting for Trump was generally accepted as true, based on exit polling. However, in August of 2018, the Pew Research Center released a study, *"An Examination of the 2016 Electorate, Based on Validated Voters,"* which places the number closer to 47%.

47 *Feminism is for Everybody: Passionate Politics* by bell hooks, Routledge, 2015.

52 Thanks to Tara McMullin at CoCommercial for encouraging me think more about business legacy and impact, and for reminding me that a business is an opportunity to create something bigger than yourself.

I am using Wollenstonecraft's, *"A Vindication of the Rights of Women"* (1792) as a loose reference point for the beginning of Western feminist scholarship. Some scholars cite feminist works dating as far back as the 15th century.

61 Maria Nemeth has an excellent core values exercise in *The Energy of Money: A Spiritual Guide to Financial and Personal Fulfillment* that I use with my Feminist Business School students and clients. Her articulation of the connection between core values, integrity, honor, ease, and self-respect is clarifying.

68 "Consider Everything an Experiment" comes from the Immaculate Heart College Art Department Rules, published in *Learning by Art: Teachings to Free the Creative Spirit* by Corita Kent and Jan Steward, Bantam Books, 1992.

70 "The Myth of the Meritocracy" is a phrase from Peggy McIntosh's incredible essay, *"White Privilege: Unpacking the Invisible Knapsack."* When I wrote the *Proposals for The Feminine Economy* talk, I hadn't read McIntosh's work in over 15 years, and forgot entirely that this concept featured in her work. It obviously made an indelible impression.

"Would it be alright with me if my life got easier?" is a coaching question from *The Energy of Money: A Spiritual Guide to Financial and Personal Fulfillment* by Maria Nemeth, Ballantine Wellspring, 1997.

75 Shout-out to Kerby Ferris who introduced me to the idea of *abundance consciousness* back in 2012 when we were making websites together. Georgia Lee Hussey of Modernist Financial suggested to me that *enough* is a core tenet of *abundance*. My acupuncturist, Marissa Mayer was an important money mentor, teaching me the relationship between nature and abundance. "Feel how rich you are already" is a gift from Sarah Fontaine.

76 My healing arts teacher, Liliana Barzola of Lotus Lantern Healing Arts, instilled in me the wisdom that "a healing for them is a healing for me."

84 This is an art piece I created in 2014 for an exhibition celebrating the music of The Talking Heads. "Never for money, always for love" is a lyric from *This Must Be The Place*. Thanks to Kate Bingaman-Burt, Frank Chimero, Will Bryant & Land Gallery for including me in the show.

89 "We make the road by walking" comes from the title of a book of conversations on education and social change by Myles Horton and Paolo Friere.

PHOTOGRAPHS

10   *Motel* by Anthony Georgis
19   *Earth* by NASA
53   *Palm* stock photo
98   *Jenn* by Aubree Bernier-Clarke

All photographs © 2014-2018 Jennifer Armbrust.

IV   *Light Hits,* Portland, Oregon
IX   *Bay Laurel,* Topanga Canyon, California
30   *Agave,* Silver Lake, California
39   *Camellia,* Portland, Oregon
43   *Fennel,* Topanga Beach, California
44   *Seed,* Silver Lake, California
46   *Bell & Blanket,* Topanga Canyon, California
56   *Your Body is Not a Lemon,* Topanga, California
60   *Aster,* Topanga Canyon, California
65   *Coast Goldenbush,* Malibu, California
66   *Century Plant,* Anza Borrego, California
69   *Superba,* Venice, California
73   *Palms,* Culver City, California
74   *African Daisies,* Malibu, California
77   *Foraged Pomegranate,* Topanga Canyon, California
82   *The Feeling of Being Free,* Big Sur, California
84   *Always For Love,* Portland, Oregon
96   *Pink Ladies,* Malibu, California

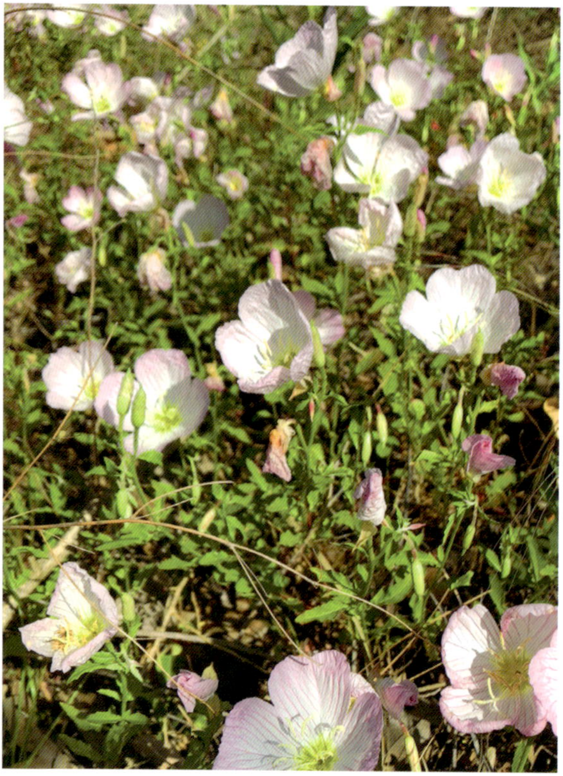

THANK YOU

Sarah Fontaine
Liliana Barzola
Jen Wick
Marissa Mayer, LAc
May Juliette Barruel
Liz Haley
Lisa Radon
Taryn Cowart
Amelia Hruby

Tsilli Pines, for inviting me to speak at CreativeMornings even though I had no public speaking experience. And for moving the venue on short notice when the audience grew to over 400 people. And for teaching me the night before to make slide presentations in Keynote instead of InDesign. Without her trust, this book would not exist.

Therese Saliba & Larry Mosqueda, who taught me how to think and opened the doors to the wonderland of critical theory, feminism, and political economy.

Our feminist grandmothers—those who are living, those who have passed, & those who have not yet been born.

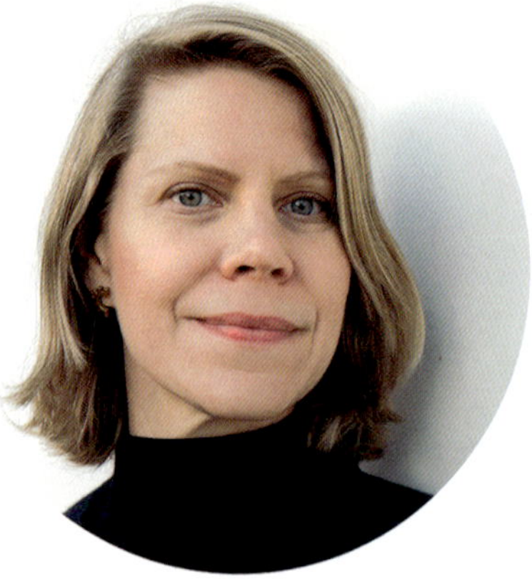

BIOGRAPHY

JENNIFER ARMBRUST is the founder and director of Sister where she cultivates teaching & tools for the Feminine Economy, practices embodied business, and runs Feminist Business School. Her work explores the collisions and collusions of business, art, gender, and economics.

Armbrust has 16 years of entrepreneurial experience, as owner and partner of five different businesses. Formerly the proprietor and director of a fine art gallery, founding partner of an online arts magazine, managing director of an arts nonprofit, principal of a small interactive design studio, and head of her own creative consultancy, Armbrust has long been interested in the intersections of business and art and more recently, business *as* art.

She holds a degree in Critical Theory from The Evergreen State College with continuing studies in small business administration (Portland Community College), interactive design (Pacific Northwest College of Art), and healing arts (Lotus Lantern Healing Arts).

She lives in Topanga Canyon, California, where she is lovingly devoted to surfing 3-foot right point breaks, while dreaming of the elusive left.

**SISTER
IS
TEACHING & TOOLS FOR THE FEMININE ECONOMY**

The Feminine Economics Department
Feminist Business School
Embodied Business Consulting

☺
sister.is